Deal Castle

Paul Pattison

CONTENTS

Tour of the Castle

OVERVIEW AND SETTING

In 1538–9, when an invasion of England by European forces seemed likely, Henry VIII (r.1509–47) made plans to build artillery forts along the east and south coasts of England. These forts were built to an innovative design, replacing the high walls of their medieval predecessors with low-profiled, massively built, rounded walls and bastions to both resist enemy artillery and provide platforms for an all-round field of fire.

In the Deal area, their defensive purpose was twofold. First, the defences would provide heavy artillery to protect the Downs, an important offshore anchorage where merchant ships and men-of-war from many nations sought haven during storms in the Channel.

Second, the Downs were close to an area of low land with a shingle beach that extends for four miles between Kingsdown and Sandown. The beach offered an easy landing place for enemy forces after only a short crossing of the Channel from Continental Europe. Foreign soldiers might use the beach to disembark in an area that was otherwise dominated by the high impenetrable cliffs of the North Downs, extending south to Dover. North of Sandown, the beach continued but navigation in Sandwich Bay was difficult, with extensive sand dunes inland that were awkward to cross with heavy equipment, while the town of Sandwich had old but defensible walls.

Three artillery castles were built along the beach in 1539–40: Deal in the centre, with Walmer to the south and Sandown to the north. Four earth-and-timber bulwarks (gun forts) – no longer extant – stood between the castles. All seven forts were connected by an earthwork rampart, thereby

Above: The Three Castles in the Downs, *a late 17th-century painting of the English school. Walmer Castle is shown in the foreground to the right, with Deal to the left and Sandown in the far distance*
Below: *Sandown Castle from the south, photographed in the second half of the 19th century. Damaged by coastal erosion, the castle was later largely demolished*

Facing page: *An aerial view of the east and south-east outer bastions*

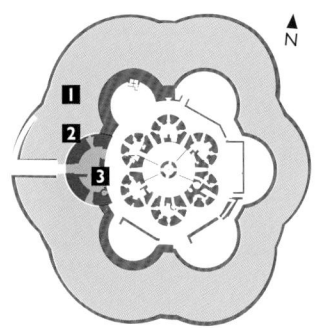

Below: The high-walled moat provided a formidable defence, not least because attackers trying to cross it faced gunfire through the square embrasures or openings in the inner wall (on the left)

creating a formidable defensive line that extended for over two and a half miles at the sea's edge.

Deal Castle was carefully designed for all-round defence. At its centre rises a circular keep, surrounded at a lower level by six semi-circular inner bastions. These are in turn encircled by a narrow courtyard, and beyond that by another six, large outer bastions. Beyond these outer bastions, a dry moat completes a symmetrical plan in a striking lobed design. This is often referred to, in error, as a Tudor rose.

◼ MOAT

The deep, dry moat, with almost vertical walls, formed a perilous obstacle to attackers. Anyone attempting to cross it faced being shot at through the square embrasures in the inner wall. These openings correspond to 53 handgun positions in the Rounds, a perimeter passage built inside the wall thickness. There is only one, strong door into the moat – a 'sally port' – through which defenders could emerge to surprise enemy soldiers.

The beach was originally closer to the moat. During storms the sea deposited shingle in the moat. This problem was solved, partly, in 1725–6 by building a drift wharf – a dam where the promenade stands today – to prevent the sea eroding the moat wall, and also by natural forces that widened the beach.

◼ GATEHOUSE AND ◼ PORTER'S LODGE

The gatehouse is part of the west outer bastion. On the outside, it contains the outer gates, and, in each flank, a large embrasure for a heavy gun to defend the approaches. A stone causeway stops short of the outer gates, where a short, wooden, modern bridge occupies the site of a drawbridge. Just above and to each side of the gate arch, a stone block with a circular hole allowed the movement of ropes or chains for operating the drawbridge from an upper room. Between these holes are the eroded remains of an elaborate sculpture: the base of an architectural frame that surrounded Henry VIII's coat-of-arms.

Left: A view through the gatehouse, showing the inner gunport defending the entrance behind the gates
Below: A limestone block with carved decoration in one of the castle walls. This may have been reused from a monastic house in Kent that Henry VIII suppressed at the time the castle was built

The formidable, heavy, iron-studded gates were probably installed after 1634, when it was proposed to replace the existing pair, which were badly decayed, with new ones 'to be filled full of ironwork'. They close the inner of two stone arches in a brick-vaulted passage identical to that at nearby Walmer Castle, where, in 1616, it was proposed to replace the existing entrance. In front of the gates, a deep slot in the passage held a portcullis that was raised and lowered probably from a covered position, now destroyed, on the roof. Five circular 'murder holes' in the vault allowed muskets to be fired and heavy stones, quicklime and hot liquids to be dropped on attackers who had crossed the bridge.

The interior is subdivided into a larger gatehouse and a smaller porter's lodge. The former is a paved space, clad mainly in Caen limestone blocks, probably taken from Kent monastic houses that Henry VIII had suppressed in or before 1539. The upper part, in red brick, is an early 18th-century rebuild. The wall opposite the outer gates contains an embrasure for a heavy gun to defend the entrance, while the inner gates are offset to prevent an enemy firing straight through both sets of gates into the courtyard.

The present shop was once the porter's lodge. The porter was an important officer, responsible for the castle gates and better paid than the soldiers and gunners. He supervised all comings and goings of people and supplies, and opened and closed the gates at set times that varied with the seasons. He was often referred to as a 'gentleman porter' and sometimes had an assistant, the under porter. Underneath the lodge is a dark, windowless chamber (originally described as a 'lobbhole or prison'). It was reached through a trapdoor but is not accessible today.

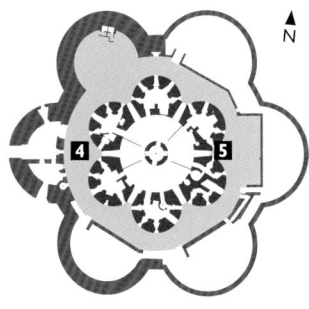

Above: A view across the courtyard looking south-west to the rear of the gatehouse and the main entrance. At the top, 18th-century brickwork caps the original Tudor limestone masonry

4 COURTYARD

The paved courtyard forms a circulation space between the inner bastions (and keep) and the outer bastions. It was also a confined space into which soldiers in the bastions could direct their fire at enemy soldiers.

5 KEEP AND INNER BASTIONS (EXTERIOR)

The central, circular keep is joined to, surrounded by and projects one floor above the inner bastions. Defensively, they formed a unit that could project gunfire in all directions.

There are two entrances: one, in the south-east inner bastion, leads to the ground floor; the other, in the east inner bastion, leads to the basement. Both have small doorways and are located away from the gatehouse, ensuring that an enemy who had breached the gates had to endure fire from the inner bastions to reach the keep. The keep has a basement, ground and first floors, and a roof with a central lantern. The walls of

Graffiti at Deal Castle

The lead covering of the roofs and lantern, and stonework of the inner bastion parapets, have incised graffiti. Many are initials, sometimes in cartouches with dates. The earliest are of the 1720s, the latest 1942. Some derive from tradesmen (a painter, plumber and glazier, for example), while the north inner bastion parapet has several examples from 1732. This date marks the completion of the main work on the Captain's House and castle remodelling, so the graffiti were probably cut by workmen. Named individuals include an 'American' in 1791, 'Charming Miss Teetsy' in 1729 and 'Gunner Ellaway' in 1940. 'God Save the Queen 1840' celebrates Queen Victoria (r.1837–1901) and possibly her marriage to Prince Albert. The most numerous pictographic graffiti are outlines of male and female shoes. A few hands – all clearly drawn around real ones – are probably from a privileged few who were allowed on the roof.

the courtyard, keep and inner bastions are a patchwork of frequent repairs over almost 500 years, but the lower parts of the inner bastions retain an original patterned arrangement of alternate light and dark courses of stone.

Like the moat, the inner bastions were provided with square embrasures for handguns at ground level, in this case 28 in all. Some of these retain their original plain surrounds, while others were converted into larger windows, from the late 17th century, to let more light inside. Around the base of the wall are the openings of inclined shafts, taking light into the basement.

In the Tudor design, the keep and inner bastion roofs were gun platforms with thick, rounded parapets to deflect shot over the defenders' heads. The rectangular crenellations visible today, built in 1731–2, are ornamental and signalled an end to using the roofs for defence by anything other than handguns. The parapets have been repaired several times, notably in the

Above left: The keep and inner bastions on the east side of the castle. The alternate bands of dark and light stone courses on the lower parts of the inner bastions date from the original building of 1539–40 **Above:** *The central lantern on the roof of the keep dates from the early 18th century, when it replaced an earlier one. The top part contains a 17th-century bell*

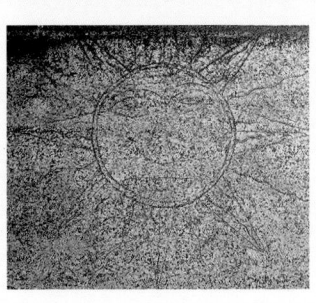

Left: *Pictographic graffiti at Deal Castle include shoes, houses with windows and flags, and an elaborate compass depicting the sun. Others feature initials and dates*

Above: The outer bastions supported the castle's heaviest armament of guns. The great thickness of the walls allowed them to withstand considerable bombardment

1950s, when the east, north-east and south-east inner bastions were refaced following the loss by bombing of the Captain's House in 1940.

The hexagonal rooftop lantern, at the head of a central stair in the keep, originally provided access to the roof. It is capped by a dome containing a bell made in 1655. Records show that in 1615 the lantern acted as a sea navigation mark for ships coming into the Downs, and in 1742 it was surmounted by a weathervane and ball. Its walls are covered in sheet lead into which have been incised graffiti, the oldest dating to the 1720s.

⬛ OUTER BASTIONS

Five semi-circular outer bastions supported the largest guns; the sixth bastion was the gatehouse. Originally, the five were hollow and open at the rear, with level access from the courtyard. The north-west bastion retains that arrangement but the other four have high revetment walls at the back, with steps up from the courtyard to elevated gun platforms. This resulted from infilling the bastions so that the gunners could have the benefit of firing their guns from a higher position, to achieve greater range. The date of infilling is uncertain.

The Tudor parapets (see reconstruction on pages 22–23) were thicker than those of today, with rounded tops to deflect incoming shot: a short section remains in the north-west outer bastion, behind the present toilet block, and in the south-west outer bastion it is complete, under the present brick one, where its rounded top is visible from the outside. The Tudor guns would have fired through splayed embrasures in the parapet, three per bastion, allowing a defined arc of fire, but together covering all approaches. The largest guns had an extreme range of about one mile.

The outer bastions were modified in 1715–17, when the parapets were rebuilt, and again in 1730–32, when the new parapets were lowered for the guns to fire over. The exception was the south-west outer bastion, which in 1733 was (unlike the rest) unpaved, and retained a parapet with four embrasures: it remained unchanged because guns were never again mounted there. Today it has a plain brick parapet and a sundial from its use as a garden in the 19th and 20th centuries.

The platforms of the east, north-east and south-east outer bastions have stone paving laid by the Ministry of Works in the 1950s and parapets of 19th-century origin. The four guns are 32-pounders, made by Walker and Co. of Rotherham, Yorkshire, in the early 19th century. They came to the castle between 1841 and 1854 and were its last service armament. Each one could fire a solid round shot up to about one and a half miles but these guns, being designed to fire at ships with wooden hulls, were ineffective against the new ironclads coming into service from the 1860s. At the rear of the east outer bastion, a high brick revetment wall is the remaining part of the ground floor of the Captain's House. This floor was designated as quarters for the lieutenant of the castle. The house was destroyed by a German bomb in 1940.

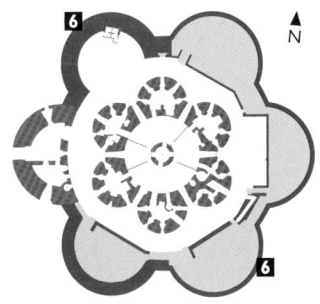

Below: General Eliott and his officers observing the destruction by hot shot of the Spanish floating gun batteries at Gibraltar in 1782, in a painting by George Carter of 1784

Bottom: The shot furnace at Deal, used to heat cannonballs

The Shot Furnace

The extremely rare shot furnace may have been built during the French Revolutionary War (1792–1802) and is shown on a plan made in 1798.

The furnace was used to heat cannonballs to red heat. The fire was set in the lower half of the furnace, underneath cannonballs placed on iron bars forming a grate. The hot shot was then loaded into the gun, using special iron ladles, and quickly fired.

Hot shot was a powerful weapon, easily setting fire to combustible wooden warships and their sails and rigging. Most famously it was used by British forces defending Gibraltar in 1782, when it devastated several Spanish floating gun batteries that were firing on the British defensive positions.

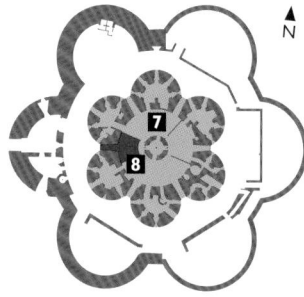

◼ KEEP: GROUND FLOOR

The entrance to the keep leads through the south inner bastion, where there are four embrasures for soldiers equipped with handguns to defend the courtyard. In the vault above each position, a circular shaft allowed gun smoke to disperse through rooftop vents.

In the early 18th century the circular keep appears to have been subdivided by timber-framed partitions into five rooms of unequal size. Three of these partitions survive in their original positions, with one moved to its present place in the 19th century. Four of the rooms contained one or more doorways to an inner bastion and all rooms had at least one window in the walls between bastions.

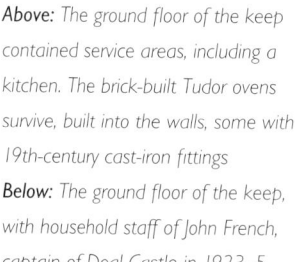

Above: The ground floor of the keep contained service areas, including a kitchen. The brick-built Tudor ovens survive, built into the walls, some with 19th-century cast-iron fittings
Below: The ground floor of the keep, with household staff of John French, captain of Deal Castle in 1923–5

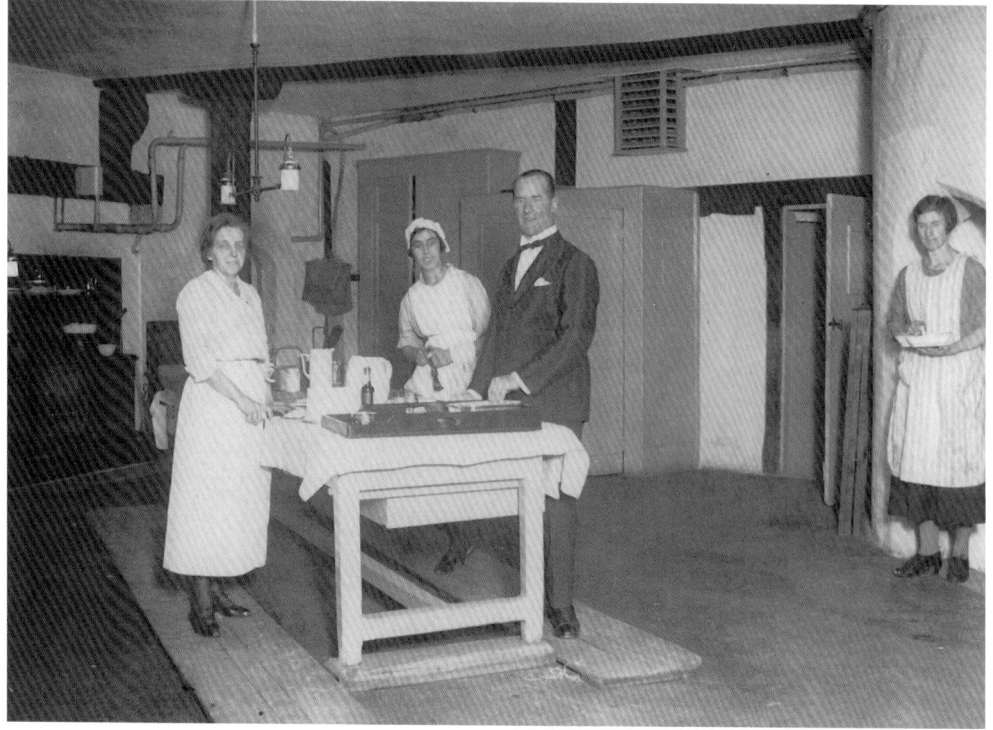

The first room was probably used as the common hall, the garrison's eating and living space. It has a large fireplace and doorways to two newel stairways, one to the basement and first floor, the other to the basement and, originally, to the south inner bastion roof. The partition near the ovens has been moved from its 18th-century position closer to the entrance, marked by a ceiling beam visible halfway across the room. This means that the ovens were originally in the next room, which was a kitchen and contains a water pump, the entrances to two inner bastions and a large fireplace that incorporates another, small oven.

The third room also has a beam halfway across its ceiling, hinting that it may once have been divided in two. It contains a Victorian cast-iron grate in an 18th-century fireplace, replacing an earlier forge or smithy. There is a section of sunken brick floor, possibly to hold bellows for the forge. A flue passes under the wall to the north inner bastion, where the circular plan and domed shape of the forge can be seen.

In 1616 one ground-floor room was used as a buttery, for storing beer and wine, but its exact location is uncertain. By 1800 the entire ground floor was used as a service area for the captain's household with, anticlockwise from the entrance, a kitchen, scullery, servants' hall and maidservant's bedroom. This arrangement remained, and the cast-iron kitchen fittings and water pump are Victorian or later.

Above: The sunken brick floor beneath this fireplace may have held bellows for a forge, used for maintaining the garrison's weapons and tools in the Tudor period

8 CHAPEL

The chapel was created in 1923 for John French (1852–1925), 1st Earl of Ypres, who was then captain of the castle. It contains a stained-glass window, dated 1920, showing his coat-of-arms flanked by British and French soldiers, a reference to his First World War command of the British Expeditionary Force in France and Belgium.

The window was made in 1920 by Harry Clarke of Dublin, a well-known stained glass artist, and features French's Latin motto, *Malo mori quam foedari*, meaning 'I would rather die than be disgraced'. The perimeter depicts insignia of Irish regiments, Irish shamrocks and French fleurs-de-lis; the background has English roses, Scottish thistles and more shamrocks. French had Irish family connections, though he was born in Ripple, near Deal. He bought houses in Ireland, at Dublin and at Drumdoe (Roscommon); the window was probably intended for the latter because it bears the arms of a viscount, not an earl, which he became in 1922, before his captaincy of Deal. It was brought to Deal in 1923 or 1924.

The chapel was restored and reconsecrated as a place of worship in 1980 during the captaincy of Sir Norman Tailyour (1914–79). Today, it is used by the Burma Star Association, in memory of service personnel of the Burma campaign of 1942–5, during the Second World War.

Deal Castle.

Lord North, Captain
Geo. Leith Jun.º Lieut.
Will.ᵐ Gimber, Upper Porter
John Clayson, Under Porter
Steph. White ⎤
Enoch Huggins ⎟
Ja.ˢ Raith ⎟
Rob.ᵗ Atkins ⎟
Tho.ˢ Thompson ⎬ Gunners
John Mocket ⎟
Mark Holden ⎟
Jerem.ᵋ Hartley ⎦

Above: *A muster roll listing the soldiers of the garrison in 1792*
Below: *A reconstruction of King Charles's Castle on the Isles of Scilly, showing typical living quarters of a Tudor garrison*

The Garrison of Deal Castle

A garrison of varying size manned the castle from the 16th to the late 19th centuries.

A company of 34 men formed the garrison in 1540, responsible to the Lord Warden of the Cinque Ports. To defend the castle properly required several hundred more men, drafted during emergencies. Musters from 1611 to 1627 record 21 men: a captain, a lieutenant, five soldiers, a porter, an assistant porter and 12 gunners.

Petitions for vacancies were made to the Lord Warden. Acceptance required an oath of loyalty to the monarch, and of obedience to the Lord Warden and to the written ordinances (rules), some of which stipulated:

The captain, lieutenant and porter could not be absent more than eight, four and three nights respectively in any month.

Soldiers were to keep ward (daytime) and watch (night-time) at appointed times.

The gates were to be opened and closed at set hours.

Each soldier had to supply his own personal weapon.

Firing of guns was forbidden without permission.

The cost of food was deducted from wages.

The garrison was immune from prosecution except via the Lord Warden.

Some rules were discretionary. On the one

forming the lowest levels of the inner bastions. They also have light shafts and were, similarly, for storage. One was used as a gunpowder magazine during the wars with France (1793–1815): it still has its copper-clad door as copper fittings, unlike iron, would not cause a spark if accidentally struck, thereby removing the risk of an explosion.

Two more doorways in the basement lead into long, gently inclined vaulted passages that provide access to the Rounds. Only the southern passage is Tudor: initially it passes through the base of the south inner bastion where there is an entrance to the newel stair from the ground-floor common hall. Beyond, the passage leads straight to the sally port, or door to the moat, and the Rounds. The northern passage was built in 1730–31 by breaking through the Tudor foundations, the only possible reason being to make access easier to the Rounds for defence.

The Rounds is a narrow, vaulted passage, built within the thickness of the outer bastion walls, running the entire castle circuit. Its outer wall contains 53 gun embrasures, through which soldiers equipped with handguns could defend the moat. From the vault above every gun position a circular shaft ascends to the bastion parapets, to vent gun smoke. Additional embrasures pass through the outer wall between adjacent sections of the passage, enabling defenders to fire at any intruders who had got inside. At regular intervals in the eastern half of the inner wall (facing the sea) are small rectangular recesses to hold ammunition or lanterns. The flanks of the eastern bastion in the Rounds contain two narrow stairs that ascend to the courtyard.

Above: This door is clad with copper to protect the contents of the small basement room behind it: gunpowder. Copper does not spark if struck with another metal, so the risk of the gunpowder exploding was reduced
Below: One of three rooms in the keep basement, with its fine, rib-vaulted ceiling. The basement was used for the secure storage of weapons, supplies, and food and drink

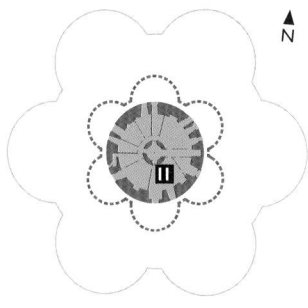

Right: The first-floor corridor of the keep, with its early 18th-century panelling. Beyond the far archway lay the Captain's House, built in 1730–32 and destroyed in 1940. The door to a room on the left bears the sign 'Battery Office', recording its use by a coast artillery unit in the Second World War

▥ KEEP: FIRST FLOOR

The stair is a 20th-century structure incorporating parts of an original double stair: one route may have been for general access, the other for the captain's use. The stair originally continued into the lantern, where there was a door to the keep roof.

The landing leads to a corridor, which divides the radial Tudor room plan. The corridor was probably made in the late 17th century, leading onto an external gallery and into the 'new buildings' (almost certainly an earlier captain's house on the same site). From 1732 it led to the newly built Captain's House but today, it ends abruptly, having been blocked following the destruction of that building in 1940.

The Tudor first floor comprised lodgings for the captain and probably his lieutenant. In 1616 there were seven rooms, one of which was for dining. Today there are eight, divided by partitions that, with one exception, existed in the early 18th century. Then, two large rooms flanking the corridor served as a kitchen/pantry and an armoury and, with large fine stone Tudor fireplaces, may always have been public spaces. The other six rooms were private spaces: one contains a Tudor

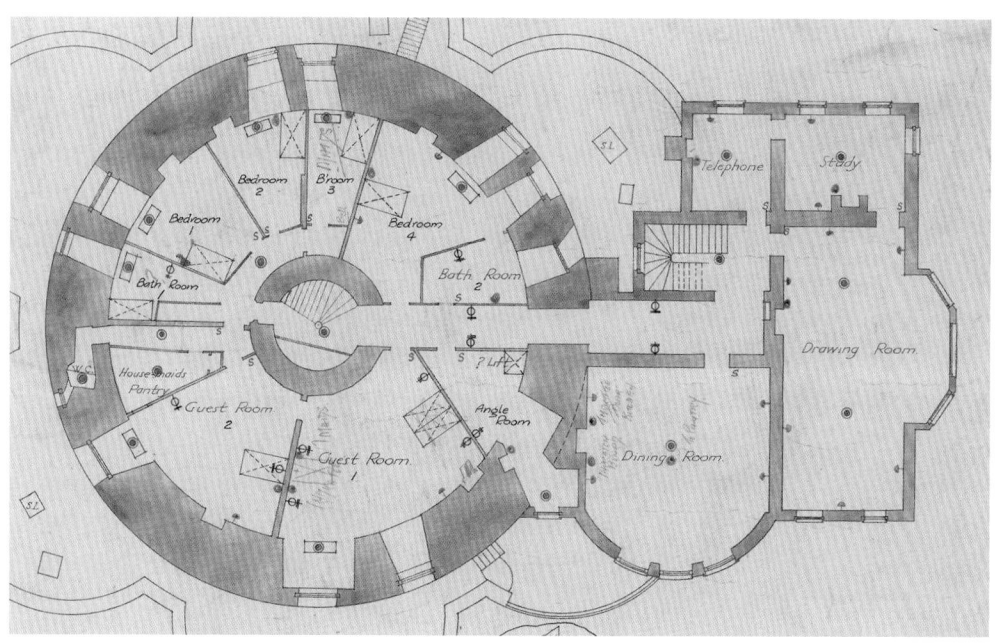

privy built into the wall and two others have fireplaces. These may have been used as bedrooms, dressing rooms and offices.

Two partitions, and part of a third, have timber frames, as on the ground floor, and are probably Tudor: one has its lath-and-plaster infill exposed. The corridor and two large rooms have 18th-century panelling and probably formed public spaces in the Captain's House after 1732. The six small rooms are also lined, mainly with vertical boards, though one has 18th-century panelling. The boards, either 17th-century or original Tudor work, are plain and set edge to edge or moulded and fixed in an overlapping pattern.

Above: A plan of the first floor of the keep and the Captain's House in 1927. This indicates how the rooms were used, and includes proposals for electric light fittings

Below: One of the smaller rooms on the first floor of the keep with a style of plank panelling dating to the 17th, or perhaps the 16th, century

The Captain's House

In the 1730s a fashionable new residence was created for the captain of Deal Castle.

Above: *An engraving of Deal Castle (1814–25) by William Daniell, showing the Captain's House, which had then been recently extended and embellished by Lord Carrington, overlooking the sea*

Below: *A ground-floor plan of Deal Castle in 1741. The captain's garden can be seen on the right, across the Deal–Walmer road*

Until the early 18th century the captain's accommodation comprised most of the first floor of the keep, with a room or two for the lieutenant, to whom much of the castle's business was often delegated. The Office of Ordnance built a new apartment in 1730–32 on the east side of the castle, with views to sea, on the site of an earlier building described as 'new' in 1700. At the beginning of the 1730–32 work, the master carpenter William Ogbourne was involved in

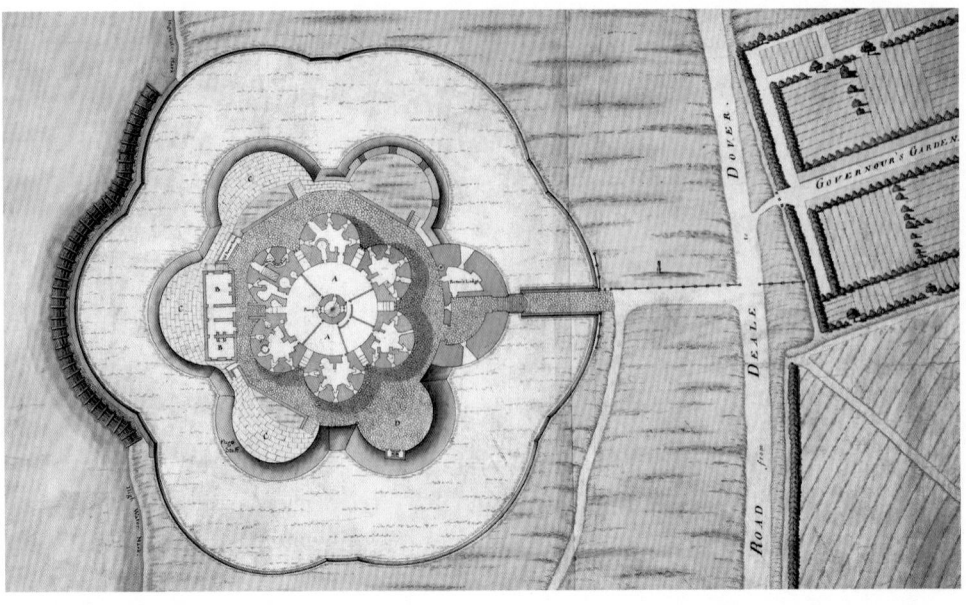

building the 'Governor's New Lodging', on two floors over the courtyard and parts of the north-east and east outer bastions. It was linked via a first-floor corridor to the old accommodation in the keep. Together, this formed a larger, smarter and fashionable residence for the captain, with a smaller suite for the lieutenant on the ground floor. Work on the new residence was accompanied by an overhaul of the gatehouse, porter's lodge and bastions, and the creation of a stable against the south outer wall of the courtyard.

The Governor's New Lodging came to be known as the Captain's House, and expressed the elevated status and aspirations of the captain, when Deal was growing rapidly and prospering from increasing use by shipping of the Downs. The captain at the time was John Norris Esq., son of Admiral Sir John Norris, who had been captain until 1727. The Norris family were friends of the Lord Warden of the Cinque Ports, Lionel Sackville, 1st Duke of Dorset, who had arranged the construction, by the same Ordnance craftsmen, of a similar extension at nearby Walmer Castle in 1725–7.

In the same period a large rectangular garden was established on the other side of the Deal–Walmer road. It had a formal layout, planted as a productive garden for the captain. The produce of a 1.3-acre (0.53 ha) garden must have been far too much for use by the castle, but there was a ready market in Deal. The garden was given shelter and protection by a high brick wall in the 1740s.

During a pause in the war with France in 1802, Robert Smith (1752–1838), 1st Baron Carrington, was made captain of Deal by William Pitt the Younger, the Lord Warden. Smith made extensive improvements to the Captain's House, eventually spending over £7,000 (approximately £300,000 today), following Pitt's embellishment of Walmer Castle. At Deal, he added a second storey, with a grand bay window extending to full height on the sea side, and a drawing room with a curved front on the first floor, built over the castle courtyard and looking south to Walmer.

Above: A watercolour portrait of Robert Smith, 1st Baron Carrington, who was captain of the castle from 1802 until his death in 1838
Below: The household staff of John French, 1st Earl of Ypres, outside the Captain's House, in a photograph taken some time between 1923 and 1925

Castle in the Downes

N

Hull Castle
and blockhouses

ENGLAND

WALES

Orwell Haven
blockhouses (5)

River Colne
blockhouses (3)

West blockhouse

Thames
blockhouses (5)

Sandown
Castle

Downs
bulwarks (4) — Deal
Castle

Netley Castle
St Andrew's Castle

Camber
Castle

Walmer
Castle

Calshot Castle

Southsea Castle

Brownsea Castle

Sandgate
Castle

St Helen's bulwark

St Catherine's
Castle

Devil's Point
tower

Portland Castle
Sandsfoot Castle

Hurst
Castle

East Cowes Castle
West Cowes Castle

Yarmouth Castle

0   50km

Pendennis Castle
St Mawes Castle

Sharpenrode bulwark

0   25mi

History of the Castle

HENRY VIII AND THE THREAT FROM EUROPE

Throughout his reign (1509–47) Henry VIII sought to further his political aspirations and prestige through involvement in the long struggle between Europe's most powerful rulers: Charles V, Holy Roman Emperor (r.1519–56), and Francis I, King of France (r.1515–47). Initially, Henry fought on the side of Charles V but switched to the French in 1527.

By this time Henry wanted a divorce from his queen, Catherine of Aragon. Charles V influenced Pope Clement VII (r.1523–34) not to grant it, partly because Charles was Catherine's nephew. In 1533, desperate for a male heir, Henry arranged his own divorce and married Anne Boleyn. In 1534 the Act of Supremacy made him head of the Church of England, replacing the pope. By January 1539 Pope Paul III (r.1534–49), incensed by this act, had brokered peace between Charles V and Francis I and was urging them to invade England.

In February, Henry began to plan England's defences. Commissioners surveyed the coastline and formulated a national programme to prepare ships, muster soldiers and build fortifications. By May, 1,400 workmen were toiling on new castles in the Downs. Discontent among the workforce led to a strike for higher wages at Deal, but was quickly ended when the overseer, Sir Edward Ryngeley, imprisoned the ringleaders.

Above: A map of the 'device of the king' – Henry VIII's great chain of coastal fortifications built to defend England in the event of invasion

Below: Henry VIII in about 1537

Facing page: A design of 1539 for a 'Castle in the Downes', showing multiple bastions and tiered artillery defences. It may be an early vision for Deal Castle

Above: A reconstruction drawing showing Deal Castle in 1540, in open country, shortly after it was built. It shows the rounded parapets, to deflect incoming shot, and a wooden bridge. An earthwork, connecting Deal to the other Downs fortifications, was intended to impede enemy landings on the beach

DEAL CASTLE IN THE SIXTEENTH CENTURY

By 1539 Anne Boleyn was dead and Henry had lost his third queen, Jane Seymour, in childbirth. On 27 December a new wife-to-be, Anne of Cleves, landed at Deal, where she rested for a few hours in the unfinished castle, before continuing on to meet Henry. The marriage was a political union, and Anne represented a new alliance with the Duchy of Jülich-Cleves-Berg, whose ruler was also in conflict with Charles V. Unfortunately, Henry and Anne's ill-fated union ended in divorce.

The Downs fortifications were completed in October 1540, by which time the invasion threat had receded. In 1543 Henry was once more in alliance with Charles V against the French and in 1544 he took a large army to besiege Boulogne. By the end of Henry's reign, Deal Castle was one of 42 new artillery fortifications built as part of a 'device by the King', in other words a plan for a long-term nationwide programme of fortifications that protected the most vulnerable ports, anchorages and estuaries on the east and south coasts of England.

In 1547, the year Henry VIII died, the castle had an armament of 57 guns and 87 longbows. Afterwards the defensive programme foundered and at Deal his vision of a castle with over 140 guns was never realized. For the remainder of the 16th century, maintenance was in response to invasion scares in 1568–70, 1583–8 and 1596–9, the first from France and the others from Spain. In 1570 only 17 guns were in place, mostly unmounted or unserviceable. With so few heavy guns, all-round defence was unachievable and the castle could barely defend the anchorage.

Below: A portrait of Anne of Cleves, Henry VIII's fourth wife, in 1539, the year she stayed briefly at Deal on her way to meet and to marry the king

DEAL IN THE EARLY SEVENTEENTH CENTURY

During the reign of James I (r.1603–25) the castle was neglected. In 1612, £400 was allocated for remedial work, but in 1615 Captain William Bing complained that nothing had been done. In 1616 a storm took away part of the moat wall, and the gatehouse and keep were damp and decaying. A survey in 1634 identified repairs costing £1,634, including 'a great timber head' to withstand the sea. By 1641 none had been carried out.

Below: A map of the Kent coast, showing the location of the Downs and the Goodwin Sands offshore, and the relative positions of castles and defensive bulwarks

The Downs Anchorage and the Goodwin Sands

The Downs is an area of sea between the coast at Deal and an extensive offshore area of shifting sandbanks known as the Goodwin Sands. Sheltered from rip currents and ocean swell, the Downs formed a safe anchorage during storms. Navigation into the Downs in bad weather conditions and in fog, however, was dangerous and ships were often wrecked on the Goodwins.

From the late 17th to the early 19th centuries the Royal Navy based a squadron of warships in the Downs to patrol the eastern end of the Channel, and the merchant ships anchored to wait for better weather. Deal pilots guided ships safely in and out, often as far as London or Continental ports.

Salvage rights for sunken ships were a lucrative business, regulated by the Lord Warden of the Cinque Ports, whose agents were often men of the castle garrison. Hundreds of wrecks along this coast included 90 from just one storm in 1703, when the entire Channel Squadron of the Royal Navy was lost, including the 70-gun HMS *Stirling Castle*.

The castle did not, however, lack action. There were frequent disputes, such as when a passing ship failed to lower its flag, or fire a salute, to show peaceful intent. In 1626 the captain of one such ship was summoned to pay for ammunition used by the castle guns to fire warning shots: he also voluntarily gave money to the garrison, so everyone was happy.

Keeping peace among all the ships in the anchorage was an impossible task and piracy was not infrequent. In 1633 the castle guns tried, unsuccessfully, to stop fighting between Dutch ships and corsairs from Spanish-held Dunkirk. In 1639, during the Battle of the Downs, Spanish ships sought the neutrality of the anchorage but the English could not stop their Dutch pursuers. Several Spanish vessels were sunk and 2,000 sailors came ashore in Deal and Dover. The Lord Warden of the Cinque Ports, the Earl of Suffolk, organized relief from Deal Castle and described the Spanish sailors as 'poore miserable people as ever I beheld'.

Above left and right: The Town and Castle of Deal, Kent, *an engraving of 1640 by Wenceslaus Hollar*

Below: A coloured engraving depicting the Battle of the Downs on 21 October 1639, in which Spanish forces were decisively defeated by the Dutch. Thousands of Spanish sailors took refuge in Deal and Dover

Right: Detail of a 16th-century painting showing a round tower overlooking Dover harbour. The gunners are firing a gun salute, as the garrison of Deal Castle would have done on many occasions
Below: Parts from 16th- and 17th-century weapons found at Camber Castle, East Sussex, similar to those which would have been used at Deal Castle. From top (not all to scale): a lock plate from a matchlock musket; the head of a halberd; a pikehead and an arrowhead; and cannonballs

The Armament of Deal Castle

The castle's weaponry reflected changes in warfare.

Deal Castle was designed for all-round defence with positions for about 143 guns: large ones for engaging ships and handguns for close defence. The largest number reached, in 1547–8, was 30 large guns and 27 handguns alongside traditional edged pole weapons – 402 bills and pikes – and 87 longbows.

A pattern emerged of keeping minimum armament in peacetime, to save money, with an increase in wartime. By 1570 there were only 10 heavy guns and 7 handguns (most of which were neither mounted nor serviceable), 25 pole weapons and 8 longbows. By 1625 numbers had dwindled to only 6 heavy guns, 19 muskets and 20 pole weapons, totally inadequate in the event of a surprise attack.

Many more weapons were probably employed during the siege of 1648. In 1691 the castle was well-armed with 30 heavy guns, 282 hand grenades, 262 muskets, 11 pistols and 82 pikes, reflecting readiness during the Nine Years' War (1688–97), when England was part of a Europe-wide coalition fighting the armies of Louis XIV (r.1643–1715), the powerful 'Sun King' of France.

After 1716 the armament was standardized as eleven 9-pounder guns, in 1733 arranged three to each of the seaward-facing outer bastions and two facing landwards in the north-west outer bastion. In the French Revolutionary War (1792–1802) these guns were replaced by captured French 36-pounders. The present guns, installed between 1841 and 1854, are British 32-pounders made in Rotherham, Yorkshire, by Walker and Co.

THE CIVIL WAR SIEGE

In 1648, following the First English Civil War (1642–6), the uncertain future of Charles I (r.1625–49) and tension between political factions resulted in a mutiny of the fleet in the Downs. The garrisons of the three Downs castles defected to the king and a Parliamentary force under Colonel Nathaniel Rich arrived early in June to retake them. Walmer Castle surrendered on 1 July, having endured bombardment by devastating mortar shells. Deal Castle received similar treatment but held out and fought back. The crucial engagement came on 15 August, when an 800-strong Royalist relief force attempted to surprise Colonel Rich at night. The attack failed and Rich's soldiers inflicted heavy losses on the Royalists. Deal then surrendered on 25 August, joined by Sandown Castle on 3 September.

DEAL DURING ENGLAND'S WARS IN THE LATER SEVENTEENTH CENTURY

During the second half of the 17th century, England was involved in many conflicts, including the Anglo-Dutch Wars (1652–4, 1665–7 and 1672–4), the Franco-Dutch War (1672–8) and the Nine Years' War (1688–97). Battles were fought at sea or abroad but the English coast was often threatened and the Downs, by then a major naval anchorage, was an obvious target. In 1666–7 a Dutch fleet cruised the Kent coast, seeking opportunity to attack. The captain of Deal Castle, Colonel Silius Titus (1622/3–1704), was responsible for the coast from Walmer to the Isle of Thanet, commanding the castle garrisons and several companies of professional soldiers and trained bands. These included the 'yellowcoats' of the Duke of York and Albany's Maritime Regiment of Foot, known today as the Royal Marines. Extra guns were emplaced and temporary defences made, including turf breastworks on the castles to protect the garrisons from incoming shot, and patching up the old walls of Sandwich. In the event, the Dutch attack was made on the river Medway, to the humiliation of the English. Peace quickly followed.

Above: Detail of a 17th-century woodcut of Royalist warships in the Downs, which came to the aid of the besieged Downs castles in 1648

Below: Willem Schellinks's painting (c.1667–8) of the Dutch attack on the English fleet in the Medway in June 1667. The castles of the Downs were also under threat from the Dutch at this time and from other European forces throughout the later 17th century

In 1672 a naval storehouse was built immediately north of the castle, to service ships of the Royal Navy in the Downs. It developed into a Navy Yard, supplying food and stores, and repairing and building longboats and luggers – the small tenders used by the larger ships. The yard reinforced the role of the castle in helping to defend the anchorage.

THE CASTLE IN THE EIGHTEENTH CENTURY

In 1713 the Peace of Utrecht ended British involvement in the War of the Spanish Succession, which had engulfed Europe since 1701. The reappointment in 1714 of John Churchill, 1st Duke of Marlborough, to the Office of Ordnance resulted in a review of coastal fortifications. At Deal, the castle's 29 miscellaneous heavy guns were reduced to 11 of standard calibre 9-pounders, under the direction of Lieutenant John Brooks. He supervised Ordnance craftsmen who removed most of what remained of the rounded Tudor parapets, built new ones and installed the new guns. They also repaired the walls and sash windows of the keep, and renovated and raised the parapet of the gatehouse.

For most of the remainder of the 18th century, Britain was involved in various conflicts worldwide. The Royal Navy was the principal agent of the British rise to world power and the Downs was an important anchorage where ships were resupplied, a role that ensured the castle was kept in good shape. In 1730–32 the Ordnance Office built the Captain's House and removed the old parapets on the keep and inner bastions, replacing them with decorative crenellations that survive in part today. Subsequent alterations included lower parapets for the three seaward bastions to enable a wide arc of fire for each gun, in 1738; a new keep roof, in 1739; a new drawbridge at the main gate, in 1741; and a brick wall for the captain's garden, in 1744–50.

These works resulted in a larger and more fashionable residence, where the captain and lieutenant could work and

Below: Deal Castle in an engraving of 1735 by Samuel and Nathaniel Buck, shortly after the Captain's House was built on the seaward side of the castle

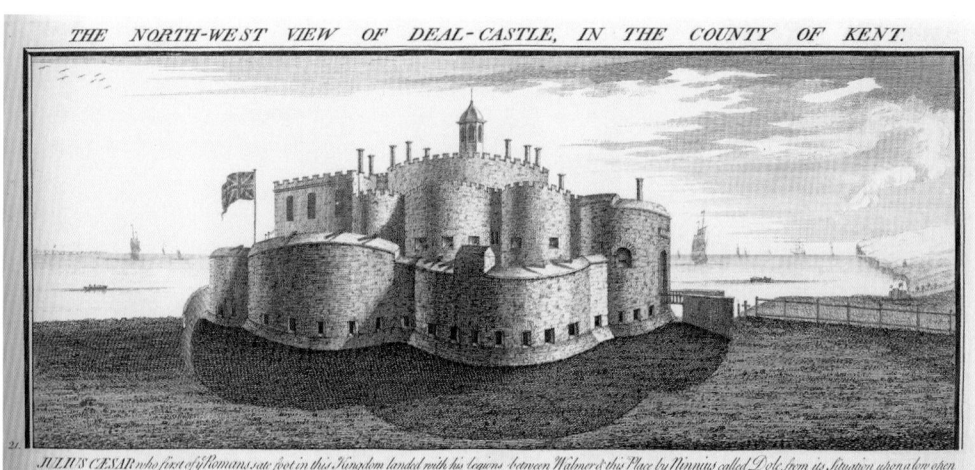

THE NORTH-WEST VIEW OF DEAL-CASTLE, IN THE COUNTY OF KENT.

Richard Watts: Government Agent

Watts provided vital intelligence from Deal directly to the English government during a time of tense international relations in the 17th century.

Valuable information about Deal in the 17th century comes from the letters of Richard Watts (1625–89), a notary, to Sir Joseph Williamson (1633–1701), an important official in the Southern Department, responsible for Home Affairs and international relations with Ireland, France, southern European countries and the Ottoman Empire.

Williamson had a network of agents, including Watts, gathering intelligence, especially on threats to the government. As a busy, cosmopolitan port, Deal was full of news and rumours. Watts reported daily on events, strangers, ship movements and loose words, gathered from innkeepers, pilots and ships' masters whose vessels were in the Downs. He recorded events at Deal Castle during the tense years of the Second Anglo-Dutch War (1665–7):

'Deale, May 16 1667, Mr Secretary, the great report of the Dutch coming this way (in time of treaty) has startled the weaker sort: we are now ready to receive them, the castles and trained companies being in a military costume through the special care and command of Colonel Titus, who is Governor of Deal Castle.'

On 15 June 1667 Watts reported unrest after the audacious Dutch attack on the

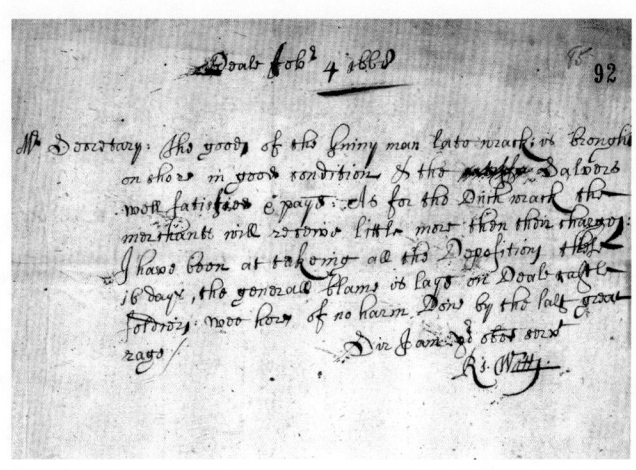

Deal Feby 4 1669

Mr Secretary: The goods of the Guineaman lately wrecked are brought
on shore in good condition and the salvagers
are well satisfied and paid. As for the Dutch wreck, the
merchants will receive little more than their shares.
I have been taking all the depositions the last
16 days. The general blame is laid on Deale Castle's
Soldiers. We hear of no harm done by the last great
rage.

Sir I am yor obed serv^t
Ri. Watts

fleet in the river Medway:

'The common people and almost all other men gather, some crying out that we were sold out, others that there were traitors in the Council … the loss of Dunkirk, the dividing of the Fleet, the disbanding of the Army, the non-payment of the seamen, and permitting so many merchant ships to leave … were called into question. And truly had not the news suddenly changed, they would undoubtedly have rose up and attempted strange things.'

Top: *Richard Watts conveys the latest news from Deal in a letter of 4 February 1669 (with transcript)*
Above: *Sir Joseph Williamson (1633–1701), the government official to whom Watts reported*

Above: The castle viewed from the beach. The crenellations date from the 1730s alterations, while the flat outer bastion parapets are of the 19th century

Below: *East Barracks, Deal, built by 1800 as a Royal Naval Hospital and rebuilt in 1812. In 1861 the building became a barracks for the Royal Marines and remained so until 1996*

entertain important officers, politicians and gentry arriving and leaving Deal, underscoring the importance of the Downs as Britain's fortunes rose. The Office of Ordnance financed these works, alongside a reformed gun battery on the castle's seaward bastions to defend the anchorage. The Lord Warden continued to appoint the garrison, most of whom were routinely involved in Cinque Ports business, as well as being gunners. It is likely that only the lieutenant, who conducted most castle business, and the porter, who supervised comings and goings, were permanently based in the castle.

In 1765 there was a tiny lean-to gunner's cabin, in the courtyard against the north-west bastion, perhaps for one duty gunner to rest and sleep. In 1749 the lieutenant, William Pocock, was also the master gunner. He looked after the guns

and stores, issued to him via the Ordnance storekeeper in Dover Castle, while the gunners attended Deal Castle periodically for training and for musters, or permanently during an emergency. The muster roll of 1773 lists eight gunners, enough to operate two guns. For 12 guns, regular soldiers and militia were also needed, who came to the castle in emergencies. There were two such alarms in 1744–5 and 1779 – both expected invasions by French forces – when militia units were called out all over Britain.

DEAL IN THE FRENCH REVOLUTIONARY AND NAPOLEONIC WARS (1792–1815)

Britain's long conflict with France meant that all its resources were directed towards what was effectively a global war. South-east England witnessed huge expenditure on new or updated fortifications, as it was again considered vulnerable to invasion. Of the three Downs castles, Sandown was refortified and two new gun batteries built on the coast to its north, but the defences of Walmer and Deal had been compromised by the building of the official residences. Nevertheless, they were useful gun batteries for protecting ships in the Downs and Deal was rearmed with captured French 36-pounders.

As part of a national programme to station soldiers at strategic points, new barracks were built in 1794–7 for about 1,000 men on the Deal–Walmer road, south of the castle, and a naval hospital was added by 1800. As most regular soldiers were fighting abroad, efforts were made to raise an army for home defence, and both William Pitt the Younger, as Prime

Above: William Pitt the Younger as Colonel Commandant of the Cinque Ports Militia in 1804, by P Hubert. As Lord Warden of the Cinque Ports, Pitt was responsible for coastal defence in Kent and East Sussex, including the area around Deal

Below: A print of 1803 satirizing Napoleon Bonaparte's ambitions to invade England, depicting him leading a fleet of washing tubs

The Captains of Deal Castle

Captains were appointed in reward for service to the country

Top: *Admiral Sir John Berry (1635–89/90), captain from 1673 to 1677, in a portrait by Michael Dahl (1659–1743)*
Above: *The English Civil War Parliamentarian commander Thomas Rainsborough (1610–48), who briefly served as captain in 1648 but was dismissed when the castle declared for the Royalist cause*
Above right: *Memorial brass in the church of St Leonard, Deal, depicting Thomas Boys, captain from 1550 to 1555*

From its beginning Deal Castle, together with Sandown, Walmer, Dover, Sandgate and Camber castles, came under the command of the Lord Warden of the Cinque Ports. He was responsible for defending the coast within the area of the Cinque Ports in Sussex and Kent and appointed the captains and garrisons.

In peacetime the captain assisted the Lord Warden with Cinque Ports business, concerning the administration of pilots, navigation, wreck and salvage: a lucrative source of revenue. The captain led the castle and garrison in wartime, but building work, armaments, stores and garrisons, were provided by the Office of Ordnance.

The Lord Warden's choice of captain was influenced by government, so appointments were political, and always given as a reward for service or loyalty. The captain received a modest salary (up to 1838) and use of the castle as a residence. The captaincy had considerable value in terms of the status and potential financial rewards it offered. This position was occasionally sold, for example in 1670, when the Earl of Bristol bought out Colonel Silius Titus in favour of his son, Francis Digby.

The captains were usually well-off gentlemen, often with business interests, houses in town and country, and commissions in military, naval or public life. This meant that they stayed at Deal only during a crisis, for Cinque Ports affairs and for pleasure. The daily running of the castle was often delegated to the lieutenant.

The first captains were local men. Thomas Wingfield (appointed in 1540), a prominent man in nearby Sandwich, was overseer during the building of the castle. Thomas Boys (captain in 1550–55) of Nonnington (Kent) became MP and mayor of Calais (then under English rule), attending Henry VIII at the siege of Boulogne in 1544. He was buried at Upper Deal.

During the Commonwealth (1649–60) appointees were Parliamentarian, including Colonel Nathaniel Rich, who recaptured the Downs castles in 1648, and Samuel Taverner (from 1653), a soldier and Baptist preacher.

From the late 17th century the captains tended to have distinguished naval service. Sir John Norris, captain from at least 1715, until 1727, spent 64 years in the Royal Navy, beginning as a boy aged 10 and rising to Admiral of the Fleet. During his last command, in 1744, he embarked from the Downs. His son, also John, then captain of Deal, wrote to his daughter from the castle: 'I hope my Father is got to the westward, and that he will drub heartily the French Admirals, which will secure the Channel for another age.' His grandson, another John, was captain from 1766 until 1774.

Throughout the 19th century the captains were politicians and diplomats. In the 1920s came two eminent soldiers: John French, 1st Earl of Ypres, in 1923 and Edmund Allenby (1861–1936), 1st Viscount Allenby, in 1925. Both men had come to prominence in the First World War.

Above, from top to bottom: George Augustus North (1757–1802), 3rd Earl of Guilford, appointed captain in 1781, in a portrait by Sir Nathaniel Dance-Holland RA (1735–1811); John Robert Townshend (1802–90), 1st Earl Sydney, captain from 1879 to 1890; and Lord George Hamilton (1845–1927), captain from 1899 to 1923
Left: *The distinguished naval officer Admiral Sir John Norris (1670/71–1749), captain from about 1715 to 1727, in a portrait by Sir Godfrey Kneller (1646–1723)*

Below: Engraving showing George Murray's new shutter telegraph system (1796). It comprised a frame with six octagonal boards or shutters that could be individually opened and closed by rope or cable, to transmit messages from the Admiralty in London to a destination equipped with the same system – the first being in Deal

Minister and Lord Warden of the Cinque Ports, and Robert Smith, as captain of Deal, were instrumental in raising, equipping and reviewing militia and volunteer troops. Both men took command of units of the Cinque Ports Militia.

The Downs became home to a Channel squadron of the Royal Navy, with the Navy Yard at Deal as its supply and victualling depot. The squadron's job was to keep the Channel free of French vessels and privateers, and to blockade French ports to prevent their ships from participating in offensive operations. This vital role was emphasized by the building of the first shutter telegraph system in England, in 1796, enabling orders and intelligence to be sent between the Admiralty in London and Deal in just seven minutes. The system's endpoint was in a tower where Deal Time Ball Tower was later built, just north of the castle.

Deal also contributed to the launch of large expeditions, including the attack on Walcheren in the Netherlands in 1809, an attempt to stop French use of the port of Antwerp. Deal was one of five ports of embarkation for a force of 40,000 men, the scale of which can be judged by the failure of Deal's postal service as 20,000 letters arrived for soldiers waiting to leave. The expedition was a failure and many soldiers died of a 'marsh fever', which filled Deal hospital to overflowing.

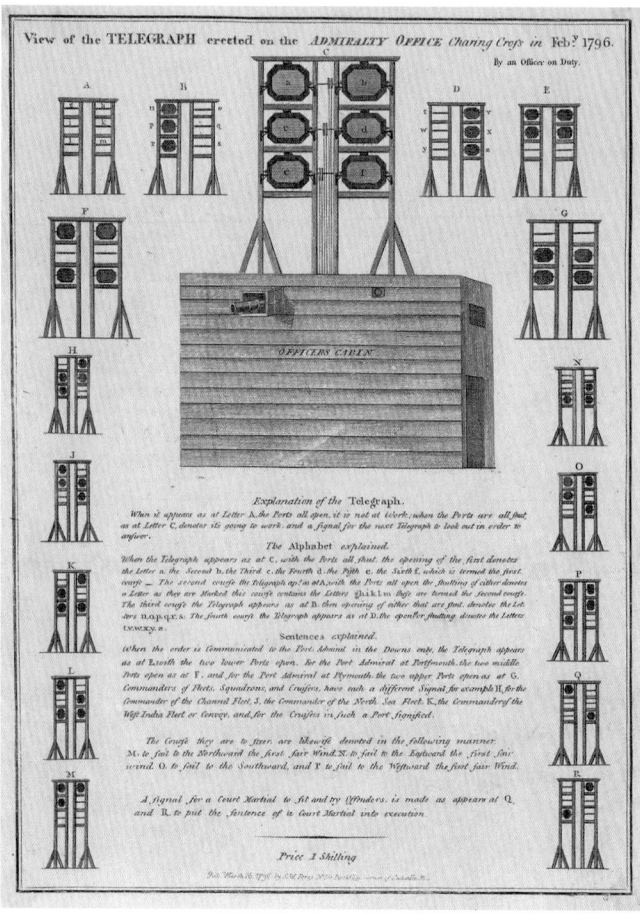

DEAL IN THE NINETEENTH CENTURY

At the end of the Napoleonic Wars in 1815, Deal remained a military and naval town and the castle continued as the captain's residence: Robert Smith, the last captain to be salaried, remained there until his death in 1838. He liked Deal, as he recorded in 1819: 'I find the air and tranquillity of this place (not to say solitude) so advantageous to my health and so comfortable to my state of mind that I shall regret the expiration of my furlough.'

Subsequent captains were awarded the honour for service to the British Empire and had the use of what was, by then, a desirable seaside retreat. By 1860 small ornamental gardens took up the south-west outer bastion, and shared the south-east, east and north-east outer bastions with gun platforms; a path circumnavigated the moat and there were small shrubberies in the moat next to the bridge. Across the Deal–Walmer road, walls enclosed a large, productive kitchen garden with a conservatory and a hot bed for forcing plants, and, against its outer face, a stable and coach house.

Despite the castle's genteel residential character, the Office of Ordnance continued to maintain four 32-pounder guns and a gunpowder magazine there. Even after the abolition of the Ordnance in 1854, small repairs to the castle were undertaken by the local military authorities until 1904.

The Smugglers of Deal

Deal became notorious for its illegal 'free trade' with Continental Europe in the 18th century.

Above: Smuggling on the Kent coast depicted in JMW Turner's watercolour of Folkestone (c.1823)
Below: *Gold guineas such as these (dating from 1784 and 1813) were shipped across the Channel in fast 'guinea boats' made in Deal*

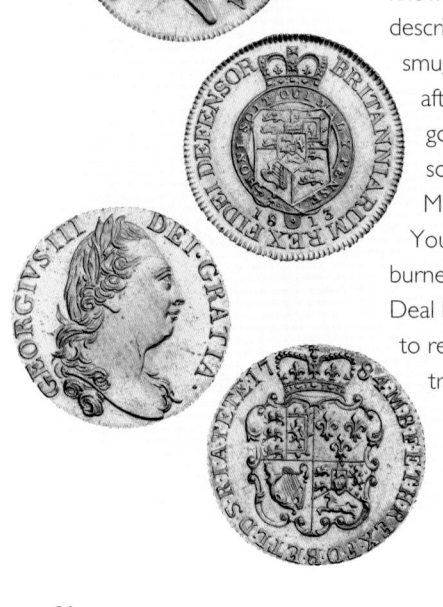

The Kent coast, the part of England closest to Continental Europe, was ideal for smuggling. Warfare from the 17th to the 19th centuries resulted in high taxation on imported goods, tempting smugglers to engage in illegal 'free trade': providing goods at lower cost while making huge profits.

Deal's reputation as a smuggling den became widely known. In 1782 Lady Hale described Deal as 'a sad smuggling town' – but only after she had bought illegal goods. In 1785 it had grown so notorious that the Prime Minister, William Pitt the Younger, sent soldiers who burned the smugglers' boats on Deal beach. With boats easy to replace, however, illegal trade continued.

Deal smugglers built 'guinea boats', fast oared vessels capable of crossing to France overnight and outrunning pursuing sailing vessels. Between 1810 and 1814 Napoleon allowed English smugglers to use some French ports. The English took gold guineas (hence 'guinea boats') – the best currency in wartime – and escaped French prisoner-of-war officers, who were ransomed for a high price. The smugglers returned with luxury items including brandy, gin, lace, silk and leather. These were fenced by Deal merchants and shopkeepers, who sent lists of orders with the smugglers: in 1813 Mr Harvey wrote to Monsieur Bonverlett at Gravelines for 40 guineas' worth of plain dark shawls.

Smuggling was finally ended by the British government's free trade policy of the 1840s, when import tax was cut to an affordable level that made the risk unnecessary.

THE CASTLE DURING PEACE AND WAR

In 1904 the War Office conceded that the castle no longer had a military purpose and agreed to transfer responsibility for it to the Office of Works. It was to be cared for as an historic building, even though it remained the official residence of the captain, who was still appointed by the Lord Warden of the Cinque Ports. It proved to be an uneasy 'landlord and tenant' relationship, with frequent tension and disagreement between them. The discussions about what maintenance was required, who was responsible and what facilities might be provided for the captain from the public purse were tortuous. Nevertheless, repair and maintenance began and continued until the outbreak of the First World War in 1914, resuming only at the end of hostilities, in 1918.

There is no evidence that the castle fulfilled any military function during the First World War, but in the Second World War (1939–45) it was brought back into service. In May 1940, with the war going badly for the British in France and German forces becoming active in the Channel, the castle was earmarked by the Army as the base for an emergency battery of coast defence guns. Two camouflaged emplacements for 6-inch guns were built next to the promenade, with an underground magazine in the castle's paddock to the south. A concrete battery observation post was built on the east outer bastion and the castle interior modified for the battery office, accommodation and stores. A footbridge was built from the south-east outer bastion across the moat to the rear of the northern 6-inch gun. The promenade, beach and adjacent streets were defended by barbed wire entanglements and concrete obstacles to counter the movement of enemy troops and vehicles that might make landfall.

Deal Battery was ready for action in June 1940, part of a rapid expansion in coastal defence that extended into 1941, by which time 31 new gun batteries had been built between

Above: Portrait of Field Marshal Edmund Allenby, 1st Viscount Allenby, painted before 1926 by Eric Henri Kennington. Allenby was captain of Deal Castle in 1925–7. He had commanded the Egyptian Expeditionary Force in 1917–18, when he fought the Ottomans out of Sinai and Palestine, famously taking Jerusalem in 1917

Below: Workmen from the Office of Works pose for a photograph outside the castle gatehouse in the 1920s

Right: The concrete battery observation post built in 1940 on the east outer bastion. From its wide observation window, a Royal Artillery unit supervised the firing of two 6-inch emergency coast defence guns

Below: An aerial photograph from 1948 showing the damage to the moat wall (at upper left) caused by the impact of a German bomb in October 1940

Littlehampton (Sussex) and Herne Bay (Kent), all controlled from headquarters in Dover Castle. In 1942, 337 Battery, 563 Coast Regiment Royal Artillery was operating the Deal guns but from 1 April 1944 the Home Guard replaced most of the artillerymen, except officers and key staff, until June 1945, when the battery was decommissioned.

The most significant wartime moment was the impact of a German bomb that exploded at 1:30pm on Friday 5 October 1940. It severely damaged the Captain's House, and made a hole in the north-east outer wall of the moat and part of the Rounds opposite. The captain, William Birdwood (1865–1951), 1st Baron Birdwood, was not in residence and no-one was hurt, but the 18th-century lodgings of the Captain's House were beyond repair. Not everyone was unhappy about the loss: an official from the Office of Works wryly recorded on file: 'Gloria

Deal. The Castle from the Parade

Deal: A Town and Port Without a Harbour

Deal thrived by servicing ships and as a port, and later as a seaside resort.

Deal was recorded in Domesday Book of 1086 as a small village, today known as Upper Deal, about a mile from the sea. In the 13th century it was dependent on the nearby port of Sandwich, but in the late 15th century ships were using the Downs as an anchorage, as silt had blocked Sandwich haven. Consequently, huts and storehouses emerged along the beach opposite the anchorage, in an area later known as Lower Deal. These were gradually replaced by permanent buildings, numbering 40 houses with about 250 residents in the 1620s. In 1630 William Bing, captain of Deal Castle, complained to the Privy Council: 'That there are diverse small cottages erected near the said Castle of Deal, to the great annoyance of his Majesty's fort

… and have taken away sight of Sandown Castle.'

In 1699, with a population of 3,000, Deal achieved the status of a town. It prospered by servicing ships, particularly Royal Navy vessels. Deal luggers ferried people and supplies, while craftsmen built and repaired naval longboats and smaller pinnaces on shore. A Navy Yard was established by the early 1650s, and moved to a site north of Deal Castle later in the 17th century.

Deal prospered, especially in wartime, and in the 18th century was an exceptionally busy port. After 1815, with the suppression of smuggling and the invention of steamships, Deal's maritime role declined. When the Navy Yard closed in 1863, the town concentrated on seaside tourism.

Above: A promenading scene at Deal from an early 20th-century postcard published by Raphael Tuck and Sons

Below: Detail of A Deal Lugger Going off to a Storm-bound Ship in the Downs, South Foreland, by Thomas Buttersworth (1768–1842). These luggers were small two-masted boats, built in Deal for supply and rescue services

Above: Lord Birdwood, pictured at Deal Castle in 1935. After his death in 1951, the captaincy was vacant until 1972, when it was restored as a ceremonial appointment
Below: Deal Castle today, looking south towards Walmer

in excelsis! The Huns have done what we have desired but dursent do.' A second incident, almost exactly two years later, took out a chimney on the keep.

THE CASTLE AND THE CAPTAINCY RESTORED

In 1945 the Office of Works resumed responsibility for the castle and made plans for its public opening and its restoration, as closely as possible to its Tudor form. In 1951 Lord Birdwood gave his assent as did the Prime Minister, Sir Winston Churchill, in the following year. He further proposed that the captaincy should be ceremonial, with no right of residence, for the time being. No appointment was, however, made after Lord Birdwood's death in 1951.

Restoration took place between 1952 and 1960, with a museum established in the gatehouse in October 1963, and in 1963–4 loaned displays of armour and weapons were placed in the keep. The restoration turned out to be a compromise. The Tudor castle retains its overall shape, the vaulted basement, the Rounds and some internal partitions of the keep. But there is also an 18th-century residential veneer in the castellated parapets of the keep, inner bastions and gatehouse, the sash windows, the low parapets on the outer bastions and the single-storey gatehouse.

When the castle reopened in the early 1960s, the Corporation of Deal lobbied for a revival of the captaincy. After a gap of 20 years a captain was appointed in 1972. Since then the captaincy has been a ceremonial position held by the Commandant General of the Royal Marines. This celebrates an association dating back to 1664, when the Marines were first raised as the Duke of York and Albany's Maritime Regiment of Foot, and served in Deal. Today, Deal Castle is in the care of the English Heritage Trust, a successor to the Office of Works.